REPLY

TO THE

Rejoinder of Maj. Gen. John Pope

TO THE

APPEAL

OF

Maj. Gen. Fitz John Porter,

FOR A

RE-EXAMINATION OF THE PROCEEDINGS

OF THE

COURT MARTIAL

IN HIS CASE.

MORRISTOWN, N. J.
1870.

REPLY

TO THE

Rejoinder of Maj. Gen. John Pope

TO THE

APPEAL

OF

Maj. Gen. Fitz John Porter,

FOR A

RE-EXAMINATION OF THE PROCEEDINGS

OF THE

COURT MARTIAL

IN HIS CASE.

MORRISTOWN, N. J.
1870.

REPLY.

Morristown, N. J., *Jan. 29th*, 1870.

General William T. Sherman,

Commanding U. S. Armies.

General:—During the years that have intervened since my trial, I have borne in silence and with what patience I possessed, the cruel and unjust criticisms of journalists, who, lacking full information or blinded by prejudice, have, in many instances, spared no opportunity to pervert facts, misinterpret motives, traduce character and perpetuate the memory of a cruel wrong.

I have refused to permit journalists, who have volunteered the espousal of my defence, the sanction they deemed necessary from me, and such as have by word or pen attempted my vindication, deemed my approval unnecessary, the cause being a public one.

There has been no period when I have not sought the vindication of my name and reputation; but in every effort I have appealed to the government, in whose service my best years were spent, and in whose keeping alone my honor and reputation rested. To forestall the action of government by newspaper articles, seemed to me lacking in respect for and confidence in its ultimate decision.

My appeals have been forwarded to the proper military officers in every instance; have been open for the inspection and criticism of every person interested in them, and up to a recent period, have been contested through government channels alone.

It is possible I have erred in my estimate of the proprieties of my case. Naught else would have restrained me heretofore, for I have possessed for years such testimony in my behalf as to insure a prompt vindication from the press of my country. Potential and gratifying as such vindications would be to me, my aim has been no less than a soldier's should be, and government alone can satisfy my demands.

With these purposes and acts in the case it will not be difficult for you to imagine my surprise upon reading the annexed article taken from a New York City paper—ostensibly emanating from a correspondent of a Cincinnatti journal, but really being the production of Major General John Pope, as the use of the personal pronoun in many instances indicates. Whether the correspondent was derelict in duty in not recopying General Pope's manuscript and obliterating these unmistakable "ear marks," it is not for me to comment.

The communication is General Pope's, save a few unimportant lines. He has apparently abandoned the hope of defeating my application before the government for a re-hearing; seems to concur with the view of the correspondent whom he favors with his intimacy and manuscript, as to the undue influence that is being brought upon members of the administration, and seeks by the publication of garbled extracts, to turn the tide of public opinion, which in my own case, as in all others, finally turns with unerring instinct to the right.

After stating, among other matters, that on the 29th of August, 1862, a severe battle was fought on the old field of Bull Run, known as the first day of the second battle of that name, General Pope produces, as evidence of my criminal purpose to abandon him to defeat, the following dispatch to Generals McDowell and King:

"I found it impossible to communicate by crossing the woods to Groveton. The enemy are in strong force on this road, and as they appear to have driven our forces back, the firing of the enemy having advanced and ours retired, I have determined to withdraw to Manassas. I have attempted to communicate with McDowell and Sigel, but my messengers have run into the enemy. They have gathered artillery and cavalry and infantry, and the advancing masses of dust show the enemy coming in force. *I am now going to the head of the column to see what is passing and how affairs are going, and will communicate with you.* Had you not better send your train back?

"F. J. PORTER,
Major General."

The words I have italicised, General Pope has entirely left out in his publication. (Court Martial, p. 31.) They are words that indicate the fullest purpose to be informed before I definitely acted upon my warning to Generals McDowell and King. And these words General Pope expunges from my dispatch to suit his purpose! I will not assume to characterize such an offence against common honesty.

My action was based upon sound military principle, and will bear a soldier's test. When I wrote the dispatch I believed, from report, our right was retiring under pressure of superior force, and knowing that Longstreet was before me with overpowering numbers, and reported to be pressing, I deemed it probable my withdrawal would become a necessity if my force was to be made effective.

After stigmatising *my* "purpose" to suit which *his* garbled dispatch is published, General Pope concludes this branch of his subject as follows:

> "Was there in the mind of any honest man, citizen or soldier, any honorable course open to him except of these two? Not so, thought Porter. With his efficient corps, equal in numbers to nearly one-third of the whole army—superior in freshness and in efficiency to any corps in the field—he deliberately states that he intends to march off, under these appalling circumstances, to Manassas Junction, precisely in the opposite direction from the army, and to abandon them to the disaster which he says he believes they were suffering. Can any words add force to this simple statement?"

It seems unfortunate that such high-toned sentiments and reflections should be wasted; but, inasmuch as *I did not withdraw* (having gone to the front and found such action unnecessary), I imagine you will concur with me as to their in-appropriateness.

There is no evidence on the record, nor can any be produced to show that my command retreated; but, to the contrary, it remained all day where McDowell left me, save when moved to induce or indicate an attack. When, therefore, General Pope says I "*pretended*" to believe his forces were being driven, in order to have an excuse for the withdrawal of mine, he does me no harm, and only compels a more universal belief in his now thoroughly established infirmity.

General Pope reiterates the charge that later in the day (29th)—when the troops of McDowell had been withdrawn from me—and when Longstreet's troops doubling mine in numbers, were in position before me, I failed to execute an order, and thus caused his defeat.

I am prepared to prove that my action was correct, based on military principles; that at no time after McDowell's troops were withdrawn (noon 29th) could any attack have been made that would not have involved the destruction or capture of my whole command; that Longstreet *was* in my front with more than double my force, and that he has stated since the close of the war, and will again, no doubt, that my action not only saved our army great loss and defeat, but in all probability saved the entire army of General Pope.

General Pope asserts implicitly that the order of 4.30 P. M., August 29th, was delivered to me at 5 o'clock, notwithstanding the hour of delivery is in dispute, and his assertion is opposed by his own testimony and by that of one of his two witnesses, and all my witnesses, who show that it was not received till about sun down (6.30) too late to be executed.

In my trial I brought forward the evidence of the highest army officers to disprove the charge under discussion. In the printed appeal which is in your hands, I have had that evidence most strongly endorsed by witnesses not then attainable, and my application now is based upon the knowledge that with all the evidence time has permitted me to accumulate, I can prove the entire recklessness and falsity of Pope's assertion, and vindicate the honor of my brave troops and of myself. It was for just such a public investigation made by such officers as the President, General Rawlings and yourself, that I urged my appeal just prior to General Rawling's death. To the President, to General Belknap, Secretary of War, and yourself I am still ready to appeal, or to any other general officers you may appoint. Surely, if General Pope deems my case so easily disposed of, he cannot shrink from the verdict of such a tribunal.

His claim that the reports of the confederate generals present on the 29th August sustain him in the assertion that I had no considerable body in my front is also without foundation. My appeal (p 50, 51) shows how he has perverted General J. E. B. Stuart's report, and also Longstreet's, and the letters therein of

Generals Longstreet and Wilcox, and Colonel Marshall, aid-de-camp to General Lee, assert that Longstreet had united with Jackson before Stewart reported my approach, and that the disposition of his troops had to be changed from before Pope, to meet me. In face of such facts, I cannot see how even General Pope can reiterate such statements.

General Pope in order to culminate his virtuous indignation at my conduct, as he states it to have been on the 29th of August, 1862, gives the following extract from General Jackson's report :

"HEADQUARTERS SECOND CORPS, A. N. V.,
April 27, 1863.

"*Brigadier General* R. H. CHILTON,

A. A. General, Headquarters Department, A. N. V.:

"After some desultory skirmishing and heavy cannonading during the day, the Federal infantry, about 4 o'clock in the evening, moved from under cover of the wood, and advanced in several lines first engaging the right, but soon extending its attack to the centre and left. In a few moments our entire line was engaged in a fierce and sanguinary struggle with the enemy. As one line was repulsed another took its place and pressed forward as if determined, by force of numbers and fury of assault, to drive us from our position. *So impetuous and well sustained were these onsets as to induce me to send to the commanding General for reinforcements, but the timely and gallant advance of General Longstreet, on the right, relieved my troops from the pressure of overwhelming numbers*, and gave to those brave men the chances of a more equal conflict. As Longstreet pressed upon the right, the Federal advance was checked, and soon a general advance of my whole line was ordered. Eagerly and fiercely did each brigade press forward, exhibiting in parts of the field scenes of close encounter and murderous strife not witnessed often in the turmoil of battle. The Federals gave way before our troops, fell back in disorder, and fled precipitately, leaving their dead and wounded on the field. During their retreat the artillery opened with destructive power upon the fugitive masses. The infantry followed until darkness put an end to the pursuit.

"I am, General, very respectfully,

"Your obedient servant,

"T. J. JACKSON,

"*Lieutenant General.*"

General Pope complacently commenting on this report of General Jackson, says:

"It seems, then, that Jackson was so hard driven by that army which Porter considered defeated, that he could not hold his ground and sent to General R. E. Lee for reinforcements. But Lee, according to the testimony of the Chief Engineer on his staff, took breakfast that morning on the opposite side of Thoroughfare Gap, full thirty miles distant, and it was utterly impossible to reinforce Jackson before a very late hour of the night, long before which time the whole affair would have been ended. What, then, saved Jackson from a disastrous defeat? Why, the very troops taken from in front of Porter when he deserted the field."

From all of which I am compelled to take the inflation by stating, as a fact (appeal, p 21 to 26), that the report of General Jackson refers to the action of the next day (August 30th) and the troops who were so "impetuous" in their onset were *my troops*, commanded by me, whom General Pope charges as having, the *day before*, been in a frame of mind fit for any wicked purpose.

Nor would the reliability of General Pope's statement be much improved could he prove that this contest of the 30th of August took place, as he asserts, on the 29th, for this would convict him of great inaccuracy in his testimony before the Court Martial, and in his official report to the Committee on the Conduct of the War, wherein he says:

"I believe, in fact I am positive, that at five o'clock on the 29th, General Porter had in his front no considerable body of the enemy. I believed then, as I am very sure now, that it was easily practicable for him to have turned the right flank of Jackson and to have fallen upon his rear; that if he had done so we would have gained a decided victory over the army of Jackson, *before he could have been joined by any of the forces of Longstreet, &c., &c.*

Now I submit that Longstreet could not have been engaged at 4 P. M. on the 29th August, in "saving Jackson from a disastrous defeat," by "taking troops from in front of me," if those troops were miles away at five o'clock, and according to Pope's testimony they did not begin to arrive till sundown on that day and were coming on the field all night and the next morning (30th).

But the evidence is at hand to show that the battle Pope glories in above, was on the 30th, and fought as bravely by my troops as any others, at least, as Jackson testifies.

I beg to trespass once more upon your time to refer to the "motives" by which General Pope seeks to establish a treachorous purpose on my part.

The dispatches sent by me to General Burnside are made the basis of this effort.

Generals Burnside and Parke, who received the dispatches, testify they saw in them no improper motive, nor aught else than I claim in my appeal and here. In showing my "motive," General Pope shows too plainly his own and has not even the *ars celare artem.*

Now, I mean to say that whilst those dispatches were more unguarded and free in expression than they would have been had I anticipated their publication, they have within them facts which President Lincoln desired me to impart to him by some means and thanked me for; they gave the most reliable information then had from the army, and I assert now, that for accuracy and information, they will bear any fair test applied to them. That they were not and are not palatable to General Pope is because they were true when written and are to-day a part of history beyond his power to efface.

Without the slightest disposition to avail myself of any technical point that could be raised in my favor, I submit that on account of General Pope's course and assertions grave doubts arise as to whether my trial was in accordance with the Act of Congress of May 29th, 1830, which states:

"Whenever a general officer commanding an army, or a colonel commanding a separate department, shall be the accuser or prosecutor of any officer in the army of the United States under his command, the general court martial for the trial of such officer shall be appointed by the President of the United States."

Now General Pope in his protest of Sept. 16, 1867, against a re-hearing of my case, comes forward as my accuser and prosecutor. In his report to the Committee on the conduct of the war, he says, "I considered it a duty I owed to the country to bring Fitz John Porter to justice. With his conviction and punishment ended all official connection I have since had with anything that related to the operations I conducted in Virginia."

The letter of the article may perhaps not have been violated but in spirit its violation was perfected, for if General Pope was the "accuser or prosecutor," as he *now* appears, then my Court should have been appointed by the President, and not by the General-in-chief.

I am, General,

With high respect,

Your obedient Servant,

FITZ JOHN PORTER.

www.ingramcontent.com/pod-product-compliance
Lightning Source LLC
LaVergne TN
LVHW020642110826
845149LV00004B/1317

* 9 7 8 1 4 1 8 1 8 9 5 3 2 *